AT
THE
PALACE
of
JOVE

ALSO BY KARL KIRCHWEY

The Engrafted Word (1998)
Those I Guard (1993)
A Wandering Island (1990)

POEMS

KARL KIRCHWEY

AT
THE
PALACE
of
JOVE

A MARIAN WOOD BOOK

Published by G. P. Putnam's Sons

a member of Penguin Putnam Inc.

New York

A Marian Wood Book
Published by G. P. Putnam's Sons
Publishers Since 1838
a member of
Penguin Putnam Inc.
375 Hudson Street
New York, NY 10014

Library of Congress Cataloging-in-Publication Data

Kirchwey, Karl, date.
At the palace of Jove : poems / Karl Kirchwey.
p. cm.
"A Marian Wood book."
ISBN 0-399-14919-8 (hardcover)
ISBN 0-399-14944-9 (paperback)
I. Title.
PS3561.I684 A93   2002   2002021354
811'.54—dc21

Printed in the United States of America

1   3   5   7   9   10   8   6   4   2

This book is printed on acid-free paper. ∞

Book design by Michelle McMillian

To Laura Baudo Sillerman

CONTENTS

II. ANATOMIES

III. ELEGIES

IV. IMITATIONS

• • • *This symbol is used to indicate that there is no stanza break at the bottom of a page.*

ACKNOWLEDGMENTS

Some of the poems in this book have appeared, occasionally in different form, in the following journals and anthologies, to whose editors grateful acknowledgment is made:

The American Scholar: "Jump"
Grand Street: "Chardin, *The Morning Toilet* (1741),"
 "My Grandmother's Suitcase"
The Kenyon Review: "The Brazen Hand," "The Quincunx"
Literary Imagination: "Midas," "Suckling"
The Nation: "Lit" (as "Hurricane Weather"), "Methymna"
New England Review: "December 31, 1999," "The Moons
 of Jupiter"
The New Republic: "Bach," "Coulter Brook," "Forsaking"
The New York Review of Books: "K. 453"
The New Yorker: "Untitled"
The Paris Review: "In the Garden (Goethe, *Roman Elegies*
 XXIV)," "Oracular Degeneration," "The Snow-Storm"
Parnassus: Poetry in Review: "Late Beauty"
Poetry (Chicago): "Virtue at the Palace of Jove"

Slate: "Roman Park, Noon," "'The Tragic Sense of Life'"
Southwest Review: "Variations on a Postcard by T. S. Eliot"
Tin House: "In His Vatican Apartments, the Holy Father
   Learns That Rome Has Won the Final," "Monteverdi,"
   "Philadelphia Zoo"
Western Humanities Review: "Creusa"
The Yale Review: "A Baroque Stair-Fountain in the Orto
   Botanico"

Bright Pages: Yale Writers, 1701–2001, edited by J. D. McClatchy
   (Yale University Press, 2001): "Deer Isle," "During the
   Balkans War," "I-91"
The KGB Bar Book of Poems, edited by David Lehman and Star
   Black (HarperCollins, 2000): "Oracular Degeneration"
Words for Images: A Gallery of Poems, edited by John Hollander
   and Joanna Weber (Yale University Art Gallery, 2001):
   "Dialogue (Giacometti, *Hands Holding the Void,* 1934)"

"Late Beauty" was commissioned by the Yale College chapter of
Phi Beta Kappa (Alpha of Connecticut) for the installation of initiates, February 2001.

I would like to thank Bryn Mawr College and the American
Academy in Rome for support that made the writing of some of
these poems possible. To the Unterberg Poetry Center of the
92nd Street Y, I owe gratitude for my education as a poet over
sixteen years, and to John Greenwood and Eva Colin Usdan,
gratitude for their friendship and support.

   Finally, I would like to acknowledge a debt of gratitude to my
editor, Marian Wood, whose stubborn loyalty and blunt common
sense have been both inspiration and tonic to me.

I. SATIRES

VIRTUE AT THE PALACE OF JOVE

(after Dosso Dossi, *Jupiter, Mercury and Virtue*)

So Virtue travels to Jove's palace, where
    she means to complain of her treatment by
    both men and gods. A month, she waits patiently,
while those inside teach cucumbers to flower,
and paint the dusty wings of butterflies:
    blue, sulfur, metalmark and nymphalid,
    hairstreak, parnassian, their beauty ruined
at temperatures less than fifty degrees.
Virtue is flayed by wind and rain; the sun
    beats on her; winter changes into spring.
    Jove's hand is steadier, now, his brushwork improving.
He is afraid somehow he'll offend Fortune,
    lose the imago, the white flower. Mercury
    steps out a moment and sends Virtue away.

MIDAS

I met a woman at a dinner once—coiffed, circa fifty—
and after the smoked salmon course, she said to me,

"You know, my husband's Chair of the Greater Phrygia Bank.
Why don't you bring your kids down sometime to look

at our gold?" I shook my ears at this invitation,
and I looked for her husband's chair, which he was sitting on,

and thought, Whoa, sometimes they'll smoke you for
    the slight buzz
it gives them, these cosmopolites; but still, all that Midas

stuff, we're completely up on it in my household,
so why not? After all, you don't want to seem backward

(that salmon-pink blouse waiting); but also do beware of
ever seeming too forward (that classic reserve).

So then I thought, To the world of commerce from
    the world of art,
I will send her my book of poems first, a modest ingot,

trim size 5½ by 8½ and ample reserves remaining:
and since then a touch of silence is what I'm hearing.

THE POET

A man stands at a window facing west,
      admiring the molten colors of the sky—
      and yet that tableau-vivant is a lie.
        Reflected in the emptiness of glass,
it is his own sleek gray head he loves best.
        In any picture, he is all there is.

POSILLIPO
for Shirley Hazzard

Vedius Pollio's summer dining room:
   reserved for the elite, and frescoed over
      in interwoven shades of grove and sky.
      Imagine a single lozenge of lapis lazuli
sixty feet on a side, a sea-blue gem,
   soothing, even in August, to the mind of power.

Pomegranate, quince, oleander, laurel,
   stone pine, cypress, myrtle, oak and boxwood,
      all thick with birds, and nowhere a human presence,
      except for that low-running trompe l'oeil fence:
a natural prodigy in the Second Style,
   flowering simultaneously, as nature never could.

Vedius Pollio is the son of a freedman.
   He is known for his cruelty and his wealth.
      This dining room is the showpiece of his villa "Sans Souci,"
      and, since he's willed it to the Emperor already,
though he has never performed any action of renown,
   he has no reason to fear premature death:

his pause from care should be effectual.
   Tonight Augustus himself comes to dinner.
      The Tyrrhenian Sea murmurs at their feet;
      the Emperor smiles appreciatively at
the sow's vagina stuffed with figs, the dancing girl,
   the Falernian pale in a crystal beaker . . .

but then a young slave's hand slips; the glass shatters
    on the mosaicked floor. There is a silence,
        and Pollio says —Let him swim with the carnivorous eels.
        Before he can be dragged away, the boy kneels
at Augustus' feet. The Emperor, thinking of Lepidus,
    of Antony, says —Whose hand has never slipped once?

But Pollio, refusing to take the cue,
    repeats his own command —My Emperor
        has been insulted by this clumsy slave.
        To the tank with him. It's like watching tufa,
this time, Augustus and what he will do:
    soft when it's cut, hardening in the air.

The Emperor says —Bring me all of your crystal.
    And with each last globe and stem iridescently
        ranged before him, he stands and pulls out
        the tablecloth, and makes a mental note
to have this villa razed, its frescoes as well,
    when Pollio dies, which he does in 15 B.C.

PALAZZO ALTEMPS

Glutted with looking, at day's end I stagger out
    into the Piazza Navona, the old racetrack of Domitian.
    So many bodies and so much living stone. . . .
Bernini's fountain sends down its comfortable racket;

those lingering over apéritifs and long coffee
    do not remember the names of Skopas,
    Philiskos of Rhodes, Antiochus or Phidias—
but how did they ever do it: I mean render such beauty?

The heat of that is enough to unsettle
    vision itself for a moment; it is as if,
    under the routine fraudulence of gold leaf,
the complacent world were flushed with traces of red bole.

On a folding chair by the fountain is a barrel-shaped man.
    He does charcoal sketches of tourists all day.
    Before him sits a young girl. She is like the Venus of Erice,
like Athena Parthenos. A crowd gathers to watch this *agon,*

the glance of the girl, consummate in its indifference,
    like a natural catastrophe, and the sweating artist
    whose hand refuses what his eye has witnessed,
conditioned, as it is, by its routines.

Where her beauty leads, he never follows.
    He does not dare. They watch their champion fail,
    the shifting crowd: dogged, mechanical,
with each stroke reducing her to a commonplace.

BEES
(a plaque in the Papal Wall, Rome)

At this time of year, the canny farmer
    is threading pest strips into his apiary:
    like Hugo Clouts, for instance, in Yardville, New Jersey,
against varroa and tracheal mites, whatever they are

—or worked on the swell of the gorget in a suit of armor.
    Urban VIII had his purposes, Maffeo Barberini,
    this symbol intended to connote sweetness, power
        and industry,
the swarm of massed strength, its sting and rumor

—reduced now to a bud and barb, a blur
    set at intervals in the cannon-proof masonry
    meandering through Rome. The locals are crazy,
scaling the buff backsweeps to harvest capers.

IN HIS VATICAN APARTMENTS, THE HOLY FATHER
LEARNS THAT ROME HAS WON THE FINAL

Through the coffered silence it comes to me,
 a funnel of noise bearing chaotic Rumor,
a chorus of voices raised pell-mell, as in calamity,
 and every horn from every Topolino or Smart Car—
 but who would have guessed that the mouse could roar?

The jug-eared bronze in a hundred campaniles
 could not compete with this aerosol riot.
My wayward children's hearts grow live and marvelous,
 careening over the nail-headed fans of basalt
 with snapping gonfalon and checkered pennant.

I look to the silences of chiaroscuro,
 where Peter heals the cicatrix's grin
on Agatha's breast. Goggle-eyed *mammismo*
 has forgotten its first language of pain
 for a moment, but surely will return,

weaned from the diction of promiscuous joy.
 Here is a naked arm under the steel blade
poised in the hand of a torturer (he
 has satyr's ears: this I had not noticed)
 by whom Bartholomew will be slowly flayed.

My calm returns. I raise the mutton sleeve:
    the hair on my own forearm is glinting,
erect in a zephyr from Trastevere:
        not one unnumbered in the mind of Knowing.
        But the voices of this world are loud in passing.

GARDEN STATE

Do you know, I heard there's a place in Bohemia
claims to have invented the real Budweiser?
Just try telling that to the behemoth in the Jersey landscape.
The Anheuser-Busch plant glows like the throne room of Oz,
after the foils and pharmaceuticals of Rahway,
the oil refineries and Swedish furniture, with their intimate smells.
Stepping on the toes of a power substation and a cemetery,
temples wreathed in a frown of condensed hops,
it has buried Night and Morning in the Meadowlands,
under the highway's buzzing reverse arc,
and will wrap a million citizens in Nepenthe
before it's done. A plane muscles up from Newark
into the overcast, bound, God knows, maybe for Prague.
Doctor, Doctor, tell me, which way is Paterson?

Bowling down the Interstate
in my plush jewel, my '91 Merc,
listening to a jive station
in the odometer's glow
as Hartford swam into view,

I saw the red skirts of a hawk
flash like an exclamation
and stoop by the freckled rib
of the steel barrier,
unspooling, in one dead drop,

toward what it had seen there
on the pallid median:
the pungent rag of a skunk,
a mad raccoon on its side,
or the bloated corpse of a doe.

Numbers scrolled backward and stopped,
or seemed to, anyway.
That cheek, famished by the air
of snowless February,
those wings, mantled on the void—

what were the crystal cube,
the lights threaded in their loop,
or song in ecstasy's counterfeit,
next to that helix, splayed
by the will's sudden compression,

driven and consummate?

ORACULAR DEGENERATION

Why, he aimed the car right at that girl!
    —in your dreams: a Taurus for Europa's acceleration.
He aimed a cur right at that griddle!
    —Excuse me, sir: we are not dogeaters.
He aimed the curl right at that gar!
    —absorbed soundlessly into the flank of the wave.
He aimed a Kurd right at that Gaul!
    —at the School of International and Public Affairs.
He aimed the krill right at that Kir Royal!
    —a blush drink fit for a sulfurbottom.
He aimed a corpse right at that gallimander!
    —a sarcophagus made of pink granite.
'e aimed a whinger, Cor, roight a' that gel!
    —The eye of God still lights the world.
He ommed a curtsey right at the spiritual!
    —but the man upstairs wasn't listening.
He aimed a Coors at heaven's zone and girdle!
    —but she sidestepped the missile without difficulty.

MYSTIC TOGGLE

The summer after college, those spot-traders were shrewd.
They could tell I didn't love their talk of bbl. and crude,

so they didn't give me the job in the petroleum industry
    newsletter.
I read *Moby-Dick* instead—never mind the year.

A freedman named Temple invented the toggle harpoon
in 1848, that the race of Leviathan

might be hunted until it was nearly extinct,
across the bottle-green prairies of the Pacific.

But the Inuit had hunted in the northern seas with a bone toggle
for hundreds of years, before Lewis Temple,

like the worm God sent to wither the swelling gourd,
invented the lily iron, as it was called,

out of his sublime anger, that another race
might be yet more abject, in the ecology of miseries.

A blacksmith (white) in Mystic put it to me this way:
the toggle harpoon was reinvented to artificially

depress the cost of whale oil and thereby compete
with kerosene, which was gaining a share of the market—

in other words, whether I read about Queequeg or
    thermal cracking,
that summer, I was reading about the same thing.

"You were bought," says Saint Paul in Corinthians, "at a price.
Who is called in the Lord while a slave is

the Lord's freedman." He in his way, I in mine,
Lewis Temple and I were both slaves—or both freedmen.

We were Ishmael to the market. We were Jonah.
On Route 22 Friday night, I saw a black car

peel out of a gas station. Jaws of light and shadow overhead
clutched at the driver, and the voice I heard,

like a goad flung aside, shouted, "What shall we do unto thee?"
That car was headed for the Lebanon Valley Speedway.

THE SNOW-STORM

Hatless, in mocking whiteface, Carl Schurz stands,
tricked by the tempest out of blackest bronze.

His basalt Negroes limp along their frieze:
bare-chested, fetters broken, they take liberties

(but not with the pronouncing of his name:
it's "Shirts," not "Skirts"). He's got his back to Harlem,

where it will snow from moonrise until morning.
Wreaths of snow will swag the tattered awning

of the variety store called Apollo Eleven,
and juke the front of Shorty's Jamaican Kitchen,

give the Lickety-Split Cocktail Lounge a cold meander,
and ghost wings to Solomon's Iron Eagle Shoe Store.

It will erase Mookie's. It will make everything white.
Snow will fall and fall and change nothing overnight.

II. ANATOMIES

LIT

The salt's gone liquid in the salt-cellar,
    potbellied, squatting on three sterling legs,
the dish's blue glass like an insulator.
    I dabble my fingers: the crystal dregs
        of hygroscopic memory arrange
        themselves, and roiled clouds, labial and strange,

race past just overhead, back to September
    of '72 and Tropical Storm Carrie.
In Falmouth, Mass., my priestlike older brother
    was painting houses, living on a hippie
        commune, marijuana in his backyard,
        and I was the innocent from abroad.

Wading across a flooded garage floor,
    obligingly I held the jumper cable
to his dead truck. A huge, inquiring anger
    mounted my arm, an incandescent quill.
        I spun and thrashed around like a hooked fish,
        screaming, until my brother found the switch.

My body wrote a script on the water,
    and I thought, *How can it not let me go?*
It was later the same day, I remember,
    that I blew dope for the first time, and so,
        whether from the hootch or the hurricane,
        I was *lit*.
        I've got scars, thumb and forefinger, to prove it.

CABANE DES VIOLETTES

Back from those high peaks
thirty years ago,
I hugged the fins of the radiator
in my dingy dormitory room
as though it were a prie-dieu.
I thought I would never get warm,
after the desolating shrine,
the far place I had been,
my eyesight scorched with praying
at the light-deflecting cwm,
the shadow deep and blue
under the brow of the corniche,
the azure of the crevasse
in its forbidden fold.
My own reek rose around me,
sweat and smoke and spilled soup,
and again I saw the bald stones
of the toppled cairn
by which I found my way down,
my gait a limp, my gaiters clogged,
my steps a faltering line
across that pure indifference,
and the bed beside me white as snow,
waiting, then and now.

PHILADELPHIA ZOO

Early spring in the era of the opposable thumb:
    one of those days when the world seems almost
      in my grip.
        True, the rhododendron still has its ears back,

but daylight rallies, and surely the warmth will come.
      See how, in a mob of thighs, the kangaroos bunch up
          in a narrow vector of sun; the broad-headed skink

looks apoplectic (its face reddens with age)
    at the gibbons and orangutans, promiscuous,
        adoze in a canvas cargo-loading sling,

cross-gartered apes! The Siberian tiger paces the stage
    of her habitat like a milk-white dowager's
        last scene, a blur in the middle distance, glaring.

But their time is brief: a kangaroo's pregnancy
    lasts thirty-three days. Sun catches the tiny crystals
        embedded in the lizard's skin and blazes up,

making a dragon of prismatic beauty.
    In the spring peeper, there are silent males
        waiting beside calling males to intercept

the female when she responds, a ruse to spare
 the effort of song. Famished with dominion,
  I wait beside each concrete veldt and flue

like *Pseudacris crucifer,* a silent singer.
 At my feet there is a child's mitten,
  laid bare by the vestigial tail of snow.

DURING THE BALKANS WAR

The afternoon sun, departing, lights up
    the woods opposite in one recondite knoll
as if to say —Have you considered the ardor deep
    in this particular color sequence, at all?

Blown up by the guns of knowledge, four walls of a schoolhouse
    stagger back, lost in the gold of a glade
(the globe's round O, the stained and variegated Mercators),
    the easy shells pitched in from a bend in the road

where the rising earth-tones, spattered sugar maple
    and burning sumac have anticipated
the human taste for cruelty without scruple:
    their cattle shot, their eiderdowns gutted,

and the brain of Pajaziu Dcliaj placed on a mattress
    to witness his murdered wife Hava's body.
Once a child read a history book in this place
    and raised her eyes to the infant century,

her mind lit up by so much gold past the windows,
    past the smell of damp wool, of plaster-and-lath
—like the haggard gold of Albanian Kosovo's
    churches, claimed by the Serbs
    and their Orthodox faith.

October 1998

THE BRAZEN HAND

Late in the day, we realized:
not making a decision,
we had decided to stay.

The ferry had stopped running;
the storm rose, and the lights
were iffy. The house held, but

it felt like playing at something:
it felt like playing house.
After the children were asleep,

I decided to go outside,
to feel the shuddering buffets
by which the North Atlantic

carried the shore away.
Sand ticked like something hot
against my bomber jacket;

I slit my eyes against it.
And when the morning came,
a house had been carried away:

the contents of a spice rack
mixed with skate-egg capsules,
each a hooked dark purse,

a barren pessary.
I turned, because I thought
someone had called my name,

and saw five cartridge casings
flung down on the beach
like bronze metacarpals,

center-fire, stamped
'41, '42, '43.
The metal had grown frondy;

each was counterweighted
with impacted sand.
The sea had waited fifty

years to give them back,
and what else should I do
but think again of him

from whom I took my name,
dead at twenty-two
off a Pacific atoll?

I stooped to gather them.
A burst of tardy sun
lit that brazen hand,

so that it seemed to burn,
raised, making me insist
that my own life was worthy,

given what it had cost.

MY GRANDMOTHER'S SUITCASE

I threw my grandmother's suitcase on the dump
     with something like anger, finally shut
of its calfskin, freckled with mold, its blush and imp
     of mildew. Now the sky could work on it:

that lens of blue, pale as my grandmother's eye,
     above a half-starved covert of trash saplings
regarded the flayed carcass where it lay
     amid a broached convolvulus of bedsprings,

a smashed tear-stained cheek of vitreous china,
     and two nude headless dolls to gossip over
her forty years' grief for the pilot son,
     her favorite, lost off the carrier.

Letters, medals, newspaper clippings, dust:
     I emptied it all out. *Why seek ye the living
among the dead?* Now decently at last
     that scorched trapezium of remembering

might fill with autumn rains and lustral snow
     and so recede to earth and its few salts
after an interval. Tooled fawn askew,
     gaping like a jaw, it seemed to cock at

the gentle slope of self-heal and wild asters
     where we made love when she was eight months gone.
I stared into its blank, flesh-eating face
     and knew that nothing would be forgotten.

THE MOONS OF JUPITER

Last night my brother-in-law showed me Jupiter,
 striding from right to left out of the disk
 of vision, quickly, at 100 X.
Straight as a string beside it were the four

Galilean moons, all rapt in the same plane.
 To honor what is nightly visible,
 my brother-in-law has chopped down two double
ash trees on the southern horizon,

so that the old legends have room to climb,
 their light ingathered by his three-inch mirror:
 Callisto, Io, Ganymede, Europa,
the complex gravity of each one of them

sufficient so it actually perturbs
 the orbit of the others and makes heat,
 like a coat hanger when you bend and bend it,
—or like the obscure friction which absorbs

people who are opposed in their blood ties,
 locked into resonance, with love grown alien
 as skies of liquid metal hydrogen,
strict as those far lights, and as pitiless.

A firefly signalled briefly, then quit work
 in the meadow. The split and sectioned wood
 gleamed pale as a bull's flank or a boy's side.
My brother-in-law and I did not talk:

he keeps his faith with what it is to know
       and lose each night, across the gulf of distance,
       these bodies' harmonies, in decayed silence;
these loves, evolved and brutal; ancient; true.

NATIVITY AND ECLIPSE

Lace-curtain Americans is all we are.
     Fragile, the routines of affection:
     sunflowers worked in simple cotton
on a morning in late December;

coffee on the sofa; headlines; listening
     to the children begin to squabble;
     and then around the breakfast table
as daylight itself grows unconvincing,

stalked by some advancing hunger,
     and, unnoticed on the eggshell wall,
     the sun, passed through the crochet's pinhole,
become, not a circle of pure fire,

but a dozen shadow-suns, a patterning
     of tumored crescent and clipped coin
     and whatever else in creation
is flawed, multiplex, past explaining.

THE QUINCUNX

The westering sun strikes a chain-link fence:
>its trembling fiery beads and net of shade
impose a pattern upon my children's
>faces, two snapshots tacked up on the corkboard

which slowly fade (a holiday emulsion),
>until at last only their eyes are left,
curious and grave, in them a double question
>beyond the web of time, the speechless gift

their lives have made to mine: *What have you brought*
>*our two souls mortal into this flesh for?*
I look away and have no answer for it,
>.   not in the light's progress or the shade's order.

Sir Thomas Browne once, studying the world,
>believed he saw the quincunx everywhere.
No part, on closer scrutiny, did not yield
>what was, to him, of all designs most fair:

the four points (as of our limbs) and, at center,
>their intersection, which is generation.
In life's vein and vessel, its netty fiber,
>he saw the first warp of his own formation,

and wrote *Transverse decussated by oblique*
>*must frame a Figure Reticulate and Quincunciall.* . . .
What do his words keep of creation's work
>and mystery? Too abstract: equivocal,

it slips them, what heaves always in the net,
    mortality, so patient in those eyes,
made, *not* created, extinguished by that,
    and deepening through disordered silences

toward the one still point of my panic
    sufficient, through my helplessness, to prove
these were not for my watching self to make,
    saved by the quincunx, the strong web of love.

DIALOGUE
(Alberto Giacometti, *Hands Holding the Void*, 1934)

What is the tablet at your knees?
       —The mirror where imitation dies.

What bird's head, what ka, what escaped spirit
sleeps by your loins on the angled seat,
mute in its prophecy and sly?
       —It dreams of the pure idolatry
          of imagination, its consummate solitude.

What have your breasts nourished, pale with dread?
What grew in your belly after maidenhead?
What have your knees, sharp as new flints, grappled?
       —There is only the silence of my body,
          an emanation of desire itself,
          in its ignorance, to be loved and love.
          The prints of his hands are on me nowhere.

What is the mote that swims in your eye?
       —A sentimental uncertainty.
          Metastasis. The twinkling of the atom.
          Five barley loaves. Two fish. Capernaum.
          The broken Catherine wheel of thought.

What is the frame to which you are bound
on heavy casters, without a sound?
       —The three dimensions of loneliness:
          exile; memory; dread of the future.
          The velvet dark of infinite space.

What cry does your mouth form itself to utter?
 —An iron mask, each eye a louver,
  whether of knowledge or appearance;
  something distracting and awkward
  the troops wore at Argonne in the mud.
  That war and its eight million dead.

What, after all, then, are you like?
 —I efface the void with breasts, belly, knees.
  A metaphor finds its way through darkness.
  Reality awakens the eye,
  but cannot be known except as detail
  which makes the space its own betrayal.
  I live between obsession and will.

What do your hands shape, finally?
The ashes of some ancient story?
A predator fended off? Applause?
 —On a stage I compose myself to speak,
  for once to summon from hopelessness
  a human object. To summon this.

III. ELEGIES

UNTITLED

Here is what the mind does
to compensate for the spiritual silence:
in the shadow of Our Lady of the Rocks,
I thought I saw an elderly parishioner's
sweatered sleeping form under the noon's
press of light. But it was a stem of phlox.

ROMAN PARK, NOON

The water, gray-green like your eyes,
blabs on in the absolute stillness.

The needle and thread of an old woman
move through a flash of white cotton

as she mutters, "Men like to kill."
A sphinx nearby rolls a man's skull

under its paw, prismed with
clear spray, and a girl's mouth

forms a grainy O of surprise
at the satyr lurking behind some acanthus.

Straight-backed girls play in the shade,
their blouses immaculate.

Two police officers water their horses
at the fountain's scalloped terraces.

A young man with a book
writes down the old woman's remark,

and the idled carousel's proprietor
reads a newspaper.

A babysitter is asleep,
angled in a corner of the sharp

iron bench. The baby is quiet,
asleep in the direct sunlight.

How shall we find our way in-
to this moment which stands between

us and a remembered future?
It is speaking, the water,

telling over each detail
with a retreating chuckle of gravel.

Loneliness is not appeased,
but the water is speaking, at least.

We will follow the glance of the water.

METHYMNA

Down Hebrus to the sea,
Orpheus' severed head
and lyre floated, singing
until they reached Methymna.

You and I were there once,
many years ago.
Do you remember?
We sat in the town square,

and I could go no further
because I was afraid.
Of what? you asked, of what?
Of nothing I could name;

something out of the past;
an imagined future.
But Orpheus had not yet
finished his journey.

The trap of narrative
sprang once more in that head,
its face crusted with salt,
its hair matted and tangled.

A serpent fastened on it,
a white curve to make still,
like Eurydice's heel,
out of the gape of absence,

out of the black envy
the dead feel for the living.
In that moment I was dead,
and you were alive;

but then Apollo struck
the serpent into stone,
like a gray forked branch
of driftwood on the beach

at Skala Efthalou,
the broken radium baths
behind us, and a farmer
riding on his mule.

Orpheus' spirit fled
to the underworld
and found Eurydice.
His head was put in one shrine,

his lyre in another.
Because your kindness led me
to that deserted place
and lifted off the flaw

that lay across my life,
will we not one day
find Methymna again,
music and poetry

never to be apart?

CREUSA
(after *Aeneid,* Book II)

More than half my life I have lived without her,
her Benson & Hedges and her glass of vodka,
fleeing down the long arcade through which flames gutter
against the heaped possessions from our last move,
a history in which no part was written for her.

She does not ever come to me in a dream,
to chill me and make my hair stand on end,
saying she flourishes in a landscape of disaster,
that this is what fulfilled her restless soul,
that I must not grieve, for it was ordained above.

When the flame had scorched her eyebrows off,
she drew a long breath, through the glowing smoke,
settled her drink, and aimed questions at me,
as though the answer to her life lay in mine.
Stiff with loathing, I did not reply.

I will saddle up. I will shoulder my father (his memory).
I will lead the little Iulus by the hand
with quick small steps, who is my earlier self.
We are a forlorn miniature in ivory,
And she is the looming shadows all around.

There is much that I would say to her now—
but I have learned humility before the laws
compelling faith in an imagined future.
I have come with other refugees to the hollow valley
by the funeral mound of Ceres the Bereft,

led with them into exile in a foreign land.

"THE TRAGIC SENSE OF LIFE"

The bus is crowded. It's the morning rush.
I'm reading Francis Fergusson on how
"drama is an art which eventuates in words,
but which in its essence is more primitive."

A fight breaks out at Ninety-sixth and Fifth
around the choked doors—some libidinal spark,
almost unnoticed, just a touch, a gaze
gone wrong, the whispered poison of a phrase—

and two men beat each other with their fists
without a word. Backward and down the stairwell
they plunge like one convulsive animal,
each broken from the moment's smeared surfaces

into a more perfect concentration
on how the other might be best undone,
after long years, the infant wish fulfilled
to remake, with bare hands, the rude flawed world.

Watching, I feel the rise of bliss and shame,
covert, defiant, envious of such freedom,
and then compose myself to better hear,
with the remoteness of a thing apart,

that hard birth, now expelled onto the street,
the slack language of flesh receiving blows—
in which consists "the tragic sense of life"
(the phrase, says Fergusson, is Unamuno's).

JUMP

One day years ago, in full midsummer,
            we drove to Berne, my father, my brother and I.
The American Consulate was down by the Aar River,
            so I watched the Swiss children as they floated by

from right to left, borne up on the green current
            of glacier water, their voices live among
the willow shadows. My mother had died intestate:
            that business would be years in the untangling.

My father was settling into a sociable widowerhood.
            On the breast of the water, the children made
            such bright scars.
Each was healed in a moment and disappeared.
            Again and again they jumped, with ecstatic cries.

My mother was there one moment, and then she wasn't.
            I felt nothing. I watched the River Aar.
I should have stripped and jumped like them, but I didn't,
            to loll and spin through the shadow and green water

of a summer day. And now it is too late.
            I've been back there, and I mistake the past anyway:
like all narratives, the river flows left-to-right,
            and the willow bank is open to the sky.

COINTRIN, 1972

In the lounge I got a good *croque-monsieur* once,
        and the luggage carousel wheeled round like the world,
        and my mother's heart was bad, and my father travelled,
and under the pebbled glass were ads for corporations,

and when she died, the Jura just watched her go
        in their stubborn frozen ring, and my father cried
        and I did not, and the flights and place-names whickered
on the board, and the times, and we never belonged there anyhow,

and one day it was my turn to go through the gate,
        I who had already stayed too long in childhood,
        over the mountains, and I never returned,
and the luggage carousel never had anything on it.

DECEMBER 31, 1999

Some of them did not live out the century.
John's plane fell into the Sea of Okhotsk;
Neil was shot to death in the mountains near Denver,
and Sarai in a parking lot in L.A.
Carl died in a hospital in Reading
before anyone knew what it was to be at risk,
and Fran in White Plains, at forty nine, of cancer.

No creature dies except with the ebbing tide,
writes Aristotle; for which reason, adds Pliny,
the moon is everywhere called the star of breath.
Bright star, were these lives somehow not worth
saving? They wait upon a turn in bed,
a kiss; so faithfully they watch us; darkling,
they keep that null space; always, they inspire

whatever in us rouses and refuses
once to love chance as though it were justice.

DEER ISLE

What was I reading on the spavined bed?
You sang to the dark pines and the granite shore,
patient, measure by measure, getting it right:
And though worms destroy this body,
yet in my flesh shall I see God.
Later we sat together and drank Moosehead
and watched a crossbill parse the cones of spruce—
a heap of gold flakes, a dark period—
and there was a sufficiency in all of it.
Then dusk came, and the bitter gray water
brimmed in silence over the broken stones.
The cottage is gone from where it stood once;
the lines are gone that swam before my eyes,
the senses' proof: but you signed the air hugely.

LULLABY

The sky is an oval box of blues.
Light fades from a yellow-painted case

of Shaker drawers, the knobs' dark wood
like night to organize day's façade.

The wrist of birch in a bed of fern
is pale like yours on the counterpane.

There are leaves of shale in the cut of the road;
their pages crumble while I read

and the pasture listens, bedstraw with
its axil full of spittlebug froth.

The self-heal, purple on its square stem,
flares in an acre, a golden frame

bought from the world at dusk. A veery
in parallel thirds throws its song away,

and the dandelion's gray head is blown to seed
in the lower pasture where you were made.

LATE BEAUTY
(Saint Augustine, *Confessions,* Book X)

A shimmer of doves over the canyon of 116th Street:
they are like the fraying of the dark edge of concentration
against the brilliance of this earthly light,
not the birds themselves, but only their images
above a winter landscape supine, withdrawn,
still undeceived by the vernal miracle.
   I have learnt to love you late,
   Beauty at once so ancient and so new!
   I have learnt to love you late!

They divide into two bodies above the broken tenement,
like wings of barley flung votive into the flame
of a hunger not yet conscious of itself.
Augustine asks, Must we know God before we can pray?
I know they are raised on the tenement rooftops for food.
They return to their throne in the north by the light of day.
   I have learnt to love you late,
   Beauty at once so ancient and so new!
   I have learnt to love you late!

They wheel in silence, a shakedown, an evanescence.
They plead with the light itself like an undulant prayer:
Not what I once was, but what I am now.
In their stalled phalanx they veer, as at the blow of a hand,
a body manifold on the unresisting air,
the bodies of my parents in this light that fails.
   • • •

I have learnt to love you late,
Beauty at once so ancient and so new!
I have learnt to love you late!

Every morning I wake to the voices of doves
in the courtyard and my neighbor's Gregorian chant:
the vulgar murmur and the music of praise.
A bull-necked male performs a little hopping dance,
his rainbow wattles throbbing. In a gray glare of wings,
the round-eyed, soiled incarnation is complete.
> *I have learnt to love you late,*
> *Beauty at once so ancient and so new!*
> *I have learnt to love you late!*

"What would you have words do?" a poet asked me,
"and is it the same thing as what you would have your life do?"
The sounds of their names in my memory:
these things have passed through the air and are no more.
Light, the queen of colors, in a hollow sanctuary.
Yet—not an image, but something in its own right, then.
> *I have learnt to love you late,*
> *Beauty at once so ancient and so new!*
> *I have learnt to love you late!*

And Nabokov writes of the descent of a petal
from a blossoming tree that its single reflection
rose to meet it in the water more quickly
than the blossom fell. He says the union took place
"with the magic precision of a poet's word
meeting halfway his, or a reader's, recollection."
• • •

I have learnt to love you late,
Beauty at once so ancient and so new!
I have learnt to love you late!

Again, again, they waver like a sleeve
shrugged back from a hand writing in the silence,
metaphor the broken halves of a single body,
rhyme the broken halves of a single sound.
Who has the power to loose them over the water,
after forty days of rain?
   I have learnt to love you late,
   Beauty at once so ancient and so new!
   I have learnt to love you late!

They wink at the eye that sees them, and always beauty
is just ahead: the reflection, the falling petal,
ghosts of phosphorus and snow in the broken meander
of cornices. Then the light retires once more;
they flee to the hand that freed them; the sky is empty.
But the prayer is in the praise.

IV. IMITATIONS

FORSAKING

I lie awake sometimes and trace the fugitive
    memory of bodies and of pleasure—
and once in particular on a low sofa
      abandoned in plain view of others,
        I felt her heart under the corduroy jumper
          beating wildly, and her gentle mouth,
            which tried to feed my hunger regarding itself

but failed, because it did not know what it sought,
    her heart or my hunger; or later in a small room
a garment fell, so that her body's heat
      answered, and her smile, in that moment's equilibrium,
      in the perfect stillness of our pretense to wisdom;
        and we did it that day so it burns in memory
        like the sweat that chased and glazed our bodies:

but it was no good. The solitude I found with her,
    which made her weep, woke from its carnal trance
as loneliness and taught me to suffer.
    Now all is covered, all is nonchalance
    between us. We have built lives, citizens
      apart. Despite the fact that this is years past,
      she has not forgiven me that I did not last.

SUCKLING
(after Euripides' *The Bacchae,* lines 933–983)

Unknowable, this source,
unwilled, mysterious,
something akin to trouble
(as when we say it *comes down*);
something akin to bliss.

Music may set it going,
sex, of course, or dance;
even thinking about it.
That first day when we woke,
the sheets were soaking wet

(a smell of just-off dairy;
the stain is there for good).
It clouds the heart-zone of
every living garment,
and finds the inner ledge,

the hitch of self which grants
release and abundance,
tingling, yellow, sweet,
resonant with the world,
intent with being called,

as when each new mother,
absent the squint-eyed true
red hunger, woke to feel
her aching breasts, and suckle
the wild wolf-cub and the

gazelle, and rose to strike
cold water from the rock,
and, with a wand of fennel
pushed into the black soil,
call up the answering wine,

and comb the tangled grass
with nothing but her fingers
till it oozed milk; and honey,
viscous, gold and sweet,
dripped from the sacred thyrsus:

and, having taught this, goes,
leaving her to weep,
returned to her sole self
one morning when the blind
gums no longer tremble

with what they seek and find,
sleep and satiety,
but compose themselves rather
for words—or else for song:
this song, votary of

blood-warm outflowing love.

IN THE GARDEN

I stood in the garden's angle, behind there, the last of the gods,
    roughly cut in the first place, and time had
      injured me badly.
Gourd-tendrils nestled and clung to my eroding torso;
    my member cracked already under
      the weight of pumpkins.
A litter of branches surrounded me, gaunt, dedicated to winter,
    winter the season I hate for the ravens it sends to mute
shamefully on my head, while summer brings the gardeners
    easing themselves impudently, showing their rough
      naked buttocks.
Soil above and below, till I had to fear becoming
    myself an excrement, a fungus, rotten neglected wood.
But now, through your labor, o truthful artist, I have won
    the place among the gods which I and others deserve.
What confirmed the throne of Jupiter, gained through conniving?
    Color and ivory, marble and bronze and poetry.
Men of understanding study me gladly now and think
    each that he might be as well-hung as the artist made me.
Neither virgins nor matrons feel dismay in my presence;
    I am hateful no longer; enormous, only, and strong.
Therefore may your own half-foot-long splendid rod
    flourish upward from your root whenever your
      beloved bids it,
. . .

and may your member not weary until you have played through
the dozen figures invented by the artful courtesan
Philaenis.

(Goethe, *Roman Elegies* XXIV)

CHARDIN, *THE MORNING TOILET* (1741)

Their clothes are far more beautiful than they,
mother and daughter of the Third Estate.
On a winter morning, the Fiacre-Clément clock
stands just off seven. The sterling dresser set,
the pewter ewer and the rich parquet
are utterly familiar, yet I lack
a vocabulary of plainness adequate
to this moment. She pins her daughter's hair,
her cape and bonnet black (is she in mourning?).
There is a gilded missal on the chair,
and, lying half-on, half-off, a crumpled muff,
as if after a sexual encounter.
The girl's blue cape lights the severities of
her mother's regard, a celestial blue,
the Virgin's color. She stands very still
so she won't be scolded, but steals a glance
into the mirror where the fabrics crowd,
their nap and sheen of penitential love,
her glance, hooded but palpitant and yearning,
which asks, across the ticking silence, *Will
I be desired? Will I be beautiful?*
It is her first glimpse of herself dawning,
and standing between her and the answer
is the candle her mother has just extinguished,
smoke rising in a desultory curl.

A BAROQUE STAIR-FOUNTAIN
IN THE ORTO BOTANICO
for Richard Wilbur

Ferdinando Fuga built
this architectural brook or liquid stair,
    suggesting a broad thoroughfare
struck through the wilderness by faith and art:

    like Queen Christina, who
renounced her Protestant faith and Sweden's throne
    and, attired as an Amazon,
rode in triumph through the Porta del Popolo.

    Today it is too far
uphill, too far beyond the palms and yuccas
    for which these gardens are famous,
the back-bred hybrid roses of the Counter-

    Reformation, by color and scent
each small face sweetly abstracted, to prove,
    in a flushed agony of love,
fit for the crisis met at the Council of Trent.

    The stump of pipe is rusty
from which senescent impulse hardly bubbles
    over the basin's lip and spills,
motion no more than a velleity

of wider motion, and ends
in a trefoil pool with a sandy bottom,
        the whole darkly bearded with slime,
begotten of a maculate silence,

        while sluttish maidenhair
in its delta trembles in a cool drench
        with seeking always to arrange
its tiny depilated black stems better.

        Counting on either side
the steps that frame it, there are twenty-six:
        a year of mossed and broken weeks
in which a question is formulated:

        Is this, then, stair or fountain?
Such a forgotten place at first might seem
        a sort of *Gradus ad Parnassum,*
but water is only taught to climb uphill when,

        over the dripping risers,
led back by labors to delight the flesh,
        to slake in crystal and refresh,
it suits the whim of human purposes.

        This alludes to no other
fountain, not to the Acqua Paola, mighty
        with all its stage machinery,
its gates and wings, just up the hill from here.

It is only itself,
descending in the mottled shade between
two trunks of Asiatic plane,
an unvisited station at the half-

way point on an axis
between the palace where Christina died
and the Arcadia she founded
that language might be cleansed of its impurities.

Water will always fall.
It will outrun its gleaming scalloped edge,
in this movement like time or knowledge
or the words expressing either, toward the ineffable,

darkly and more darkly
calling up, against remembered faith,
insinuations of the earth
to cool the fevers of the mortal body.

COULTER BROOK

for Lou Werner and Elena Lilis

It never cooled the iron of a plough,
plunged in to make the water boil and shriek.
It never tempered human purposes.
There was a Coulter; he lived up the road.
He gave this Catskill mountain brook his name,
but he was never more than what he did.
Coulter put coulter to the earth and died.
Rounding a curve on spinning wheels of silver,
the vowels of water have forgotten him.
Past useful boneset pleasantly it hurries,
past joe-pye weed, forget-me-not and nightshade,
the fields beyond cut into sheaf and stook;
past Coulter's house, about a mile from here.
Incline your head and listen to it now.

THREE FOR MUSIC

I. MONTEVERDI

I came to the opera with my fingers smelling of gasoline,
having fuelled the night-black coach in which I travelled
to hear Melanto sing of the raptures of love,
confident that Ulysses would never return home.

I came to the opera with my fingers smelling of her—
not any common she on the lawn outside,
nor yet a goddess, white breasts in a golden bustier,
but the abstract smile that shadows all my days.

I came to the opera with my fingers smelling of music:
dragon's blood, mastic in tears, spirits of wine,
each note placed like a rose-petal by a vamp of ash,
so that I hardly dared look in her face.

I came to the opera with my fingers smelling of mortality;
and Time, a character in that pageant, said Let me wipe them
(for death will fit me as my hand fits the violin's neck),
and I said No, for how else except in time

is music ever delivered from the silence?

2. BACH

for Peter Flanders

Through an upstairs window, the afternoon sun
        catches the honeyed curve of a cello's scroll.
Outside, it's as if a limousine
        had nosed to a halt deep in a saffron shoal

of daylilies, the way they shiver so
        against the chrome bumper of an absence.
I want to know where that dark car's getting to.
        Grandpa plays Bach. The lovely involutions

lead nowhere, though: music refers to music.
        The freckled flowers and slant beam are not altered,
not by this. He stops. Silence starts to tick,
        and day moves slowly past its own heated

smell. His twin jam jars gleam, water and bourbon.
        A door slams, and ambition's transit now,
to which the self has given its inflection,
        stoops to its discipline of growing shadow.

3. K. 453

On May 27, 1784,
      as he followed Vienna's back streets home,
Mozart paused, startled, by a pet shop door
      and listened to the allegretto theme

from his own piano concerto in G Major
      repeated by a starling in a cage.
He'd written it only five weeks before—
      had God given them both the same message?

He counted out thirty-four copper kreuzer.
      Pleasure was like the iridescent sheen
in the dark plumage: an imagination livelier,
      perhaps, more fecund and ready than his own!

He entered this in his new quarto accounts ledger,
      but where the price should go, he wrote the tune
instead—transcribed it a second time, rather—
      and then, in his small hand, wrote *Das war schön.*

VARIATIONS ON A POSTCARD BY T. S. ELIOT
(Lausanne, December 1921)

This is a very quiet town,
except when the children come downhill
on scooters over the cobbles.
Mostly banks and chocolate shops.
Good orchestra plays "The Love Nest."
A horse fell down yesterday;
one cannot see the mountains, too foggy.

Not particularly fond of children or mountains,
one feels rather foggy.
The town orchestra played "The Love Nest"
with a splash like horse's blood over cobbles.
Then past the chocolate shops
came banked scooters through the quiet.

The horse's feet were planted in fog,
and the banks, of course, were quiet.
There were scooters outside the chocolate shops.
It is all downhill from the orchestra to the love nest,
I suppose, over cobbles quarried from the mountains.
The children—I forget where they play.

The mountains have the shoulders of a horse.
One can never see the love nest,
but the children have all ended in banks.
The town shines like an orchestra
in tones of chocolate and fog,
or like the quiet cobbles.

IN THE HOUSE OF THE SOUL

Plus au fond, tout au fond, dans la Maison de l'Ame,
Où vont et viennent et s'asseoient autour d'un feu
Les Passions avec leurs visages de femme.

—GEORGES RODENBACH, "LE VOYAGE DANS LES YEUX"

Inside the House of the Soul, the Passions wander about,
    beautiful women who are dressed all in silk
and with sapphires wound into their hair.
From the door of the house to deep within it,
they govern every hall and chamber,
    and nights, in the largest, when their blood is hot,
with their hair down, they dance and drink.

    Outside the rooms, poorly dressed and pale,
        their clothes the relics of bygone eras,
the Virtues wander about and bitterly
listen to the drunken courtesans at their revel.
They press their faces to the glass and see,
    silently and full of trouble,
the lights, the jewelry, the dance and its flowers.

(Constantine Cavafy)

NOTES

"Posillipo"
The incident described here is taken from Cassius Dio's *Roman History*, 54:23. Posillipo is now a suburb of Naples; the name is said to derive from the Greek name of Vedius Pollio's villa, Pausilypon ("pause from care").

"The Snow-Storm"
Carl Schurz (1829–1906) was a German-born American statesman, newspaper editor, reformer and political leader. There is a statue of him at West 116th Street and Morningside Drive in Manhattan.

"During the Balkans War"
The poem is set in upstate New York.

"Methymna"
The village of this name lies on the north coast of the Greek island of Lesbos (Mytilene).

" 'The Tragic Sense of Life' "
The book referred to is *The Idea of a Theater* (1949) by Francis
Fergusson. Miguel de Unamuno (1864–1936) was a Spanish
existentialist philosopher.

"Cointrin, 1972"
The poem is set in the airport of Geneva, Switzerland.

"A Baroque Stair-Fountain in the Orto Botanico"
The fountain is in the Botanical Garden, or Orto Botanico, in
Rome.

"K. 453"
The episode recounted is found in Marcia Davenport's biography
of Mozart. *Das war schön* means "That was pleasing."

ABOUT THE AUTHOR

Karl Kirchwey is the author of three widely praised previous collections: *A Wandering Island* (1990), which won the Poetry Society of America's Norma Farber First Book Award; *Those I Guard* (1993), which Richard Wilbur called "finely contemplative . . . distinctive and distinguished"; and *The Engrafted Word* (1998), which was named a *New York Times* Notable Book. Kirchwey, who won the Rome Prize in Literature of the American Academy of Arts and Letters in 1994 and the *Paris Review* Prize for Poetic Drama in 1997, has received grants from the Ingram Merrill and the John Simon Guggenheim foundations and from the National Endowment for the Arts.

For thirteen years, Kirchwey served as director of the Unterberg Poetry Center of New York's 92nd Street Y. He is currently director of Creative Writing and Senior Lecturer in the Arts at Bryn Mawr College.

Kirchwey makes his home in New York City with his wife and their two children.